Dd

ABCChDEFGH
IJKLLLMNÑOP
QRSTUVWXYZ

abcchdefgh
ijklllmnñop
qrstuvwxyz

Dalila

Dalila y Diego

Cathy Camarena, M.Ed., and Gloria B. Ruff, M.Ed.

Consulting Editors
Lourdes Flores-Hanson, M.S.E., and Gloria Rosso-White

www.capstoneclassroom.com

Dalila y Diego © 2006 by Abdo Consulting Group, Inc. International copyrights reserved in all countries. This version distributed and published by Capstone Classroom © 2016 with the permission of ABDO. No part of this book may be reproduced in any form without written permission from the publisher. SandCastle™ is a trademark and logo of ABDO Publishing Company.

Credits
Curriculum Coordinator: Nancy Tuminelly
Cover and Interior Design and Production: Mighty Media
Child Photography: Steven Wewerka, Wewerka Photography
Photo Credits: AbleStock, Brand X Pictures, Comstock, Photodisc

ISBN 978-1-4966-0327-2 (paperback)

Printed in the United States of America.
873

SandCastle™ books are created by a professional team of educators, reading specialists, and content developers around five essential components that include phonemic awareness, phonics, vocabulary, text comprehension, and fluency. All books are written, reviewed, and leveled for guided and early intervention reading, and designed for use in shared, guided, and independent reading and writing activities to support a balanced approach to literacy instruction.

SandCastle Level: Beginning

Diego

delantal

dinero

dedos

dulces

Este es un .

Aquí hay   .

Aquí hay   .

Estos son .

Este es el **10**.

Dalila tiene dinero.

Dalila tiene un quarter.

18

Diego tiene un delantal.

Hay verduras y frutas en el delantal.

20

El delantal tiene bolsillos.

Hay dinero en los bolsillos.

¿Cuáles de estas cosas comienzan con **d**?

Más palabras que comienzan con d

dados

dálmata

diente

doce

dominó

About SandCastle™

A professional team of educators, reading specialists, and content developers created the SandCastle™ series to support young readers as they develop reading skills and strategies and increase their general knowledge. The SandCastle™ series has four levels that correspond to early literacy development in young children. The levels are provided to help teachers and parents select the appropriate books for young readers.

Emerging Readers
(no flags)

Beginning Readers
(1 flag)

Transitional Readers
(2 flags)

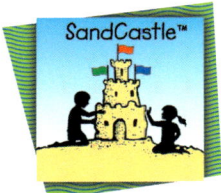

Fluent Readers
(3 flags)

These levels are meant only as a guide. All levels are subject to change.

www.abdopub.com

capstone

www.capstoneclassroom.com